Brad Pitt

Andy Croft

Published in association with The Basic Skills Agency

Hodder & Stoughton

A MEMBER OF THE HODDER HEADLINE GROUP

Acknowledgements
Cover: All Action Pictures Ltd

Photos: p. iv © Camilla Morandi/REX FEATURES; p. 7 © Cesare Bonazza/REX FEATURES; pp. 12, 15, 17 © BFI Stills; p. 19 © Tony Kyriacou/REX FEATURES; p. 23 © Alex Oliveira/REX FEATURES.

Orders; please contact Bookpoint Ltd, 130 Milton Park, Abingdon, Oxon OX14 4SB. Telephone (44) 01235 827720, Fax: (44) 01235 400454. Lines are open from 9.00–6.00, Monday to Saturday, with a 24 hour message answering service. You can also order through our website www.hodderheadline.co.uk

British Library Cataloguing in Publication Data
A catalogue record for this title is available from the British Library

ISBN 0 340 87659 X

First published 2003
Impression number   10 9 8 7 6 5 4 3 2 1
Year   2007 2206 2005 2004 2003

Copyright © 2003 Andy Croft

Typeset by SX Composing DTP, Rayleigh, Essex.
Printed in Great Britain for Hodder & Stoughton Educational, a division of Hodder Headline, 338 Euston Road, London NW1 3BH by Bath Press Ltd, Bath.

Contents

Brad Pitt.

1   The Sexiest Man in the World

He is good-looking.
He is world famous.
He is talented.
He is rich.

He is one of the greatest film-actors
in the world.
He has appeared in over 30 films.
He earns 17 million dollars a film.
He nearly won an Oscar for two of his films.
Film-goers have voted him
one of the top 100 film stars of all time.
They have voted him one of
the 100 sexiest film stars of all time.
They have voted him the Sexiest Man Alive.

Men want to be like him.
Women want to be with him.

His name is Brad Pitt.

2   A Star is Born

William Bradley Pitt
was born on 18 December 1963
in Shawnee, Oklahoma, USA.

His father Bill worked for a truck company.
His mother Jane worked at a school.

Brad is the eldest of three children.
He has a younger brother called Doug
and a younger sister called Julie.

When Brad was a child,
the family moved to Springfield, Missouri.
They were a very religious family.
They went to their local Baptist church.
The Pitt family still live in Springfield.

Brad went to Kickapoo High School.
He was good at tennis and basketball.
He was in the school choir.
He acted in school plays.
He learned to play the guitar.
The other kids called him 'The Pittler'.
He was voted 'Best Dressed Student'.
Lots of girls wanted to
go out with young Brad.
He was in a band called 'The Brief Boys'.
They sang in just their underpants!
He had an old car called 'Runaround Sue'.

Brad did well at school.
When he was 19,
Brad went to the University of Missouri.
He studied Journalism and Advertising.
But Brad never finished his course.
Two weeks before the end of his course,
he decided to leave university.
Brad told his parents he was
going to study at art college.
But he had other plans.
He wanted to be a film star.
He jumped in 'Runaround Sue'
and drove all the way to California.

3 Hollywood

There are lots of stars in Hollywood.
Lots of people in Hollywood
dream of becoming stars.
Most people never make it.
You need luck, talent and good looks.
Brad Pitt had all three.

When Brad arrived in Hollywood,
he only had 325 dollars.
He had to find a job.
He started at the bottom.
His first job was handing out free cigarettes
in the street.
He worked as a life-guard.
He worked as a bus boy.
He moved fridges.
He was paid to look after strippers.
He even had a job dressed up as a chicken.

All the money Brad earned
was spent on acting lessons.
Roy London taught him how to act.
He helped him find an agent.
Soon Brad was good enough
to apply for acting jobs.

His first part came in 1987.
Brad was in a crowd scene
in a film called *Less Than Zero*.
He was a waiter in a film called
No Man's Land.

But these were only small parts.
Brad still wanted to be a star.

4 Television

Brad decided to forget movies for a while.
Instead he tried to get parts in TV.
He went for lots of auditions.

In 1987, Brad got his first real break.
He was given a small part
in the TV soap opera *Dallas*.
He only appeared in three episodes.
But it was a start.
Then he was in a day-time soap
called *Another World*.
He was in a sit-com called *Growing Pains*
(Leonardo DiCaprio was also in it).
He was in an action-thriller
called *21 Jump Street*
(Johnny Depp was also in it).

Brad with Shalane McCall. Brad played her boyfriend in *Dallas*.

He was in the TV drama *Thirtysomethings*.
He was in a high-school comedy
called *Head of the Class*.
He was in a horror series called
Tales from the Crypt.
He was given a series of his own
called *Glory Days*.
But it only lasted six episodes.

Brad was well-known.
But he wasn't a star.
Yet.

Then in 1988, Brad was asked to star
in a Levi's jeans advert.
He played a prisoner trying to escape.
He took his jeans off and tied them
to the bars of his cell
so he could climb out.
The advert was very popular.
Thanks to Brad Pitt.
His face (and his body) were now
famous all over the world.
Not many people knew his name.
But they soon would.

5 Low-budget Movies

Thanks to the jeans advert
Hollywood directors started offering
Brad small parts in films.
They were motly low-budget films,
made for television.

He played a basketball star
in a horror-comedy
called *Cutting Glass*.

He played a child-killer
in a made-for-TV film called
A Stoning in Fulham County.

He played a student in a comedy
called *Happy Together*.

He played a cameraman in a TV movie
called *The Image*.

He played an athlete in a drama
called *Across the Tracks*.

He played a drug-addict and killer
in a TV movie called
Too Young to Die?
(David Duchovny and Juliette Lewis
were also in it.)

No one remembers anything about these films now.
Except that Brad Pitt was in them.

6 *Thelma and Louise*

In 1991, Brad was given
a small part in a new film.
It was a road-movie called *Thelma and Louise*.
The stars were Geena Davies
and Susan Sarandon.

In the film, the two main characters
were driving across the USA.
They were looking for happiness.
But then they met Brad Pitt.
He played a cowboy thief called JD.
He stole all their money.
He was arrested.
But Thelma and Louise were in trouble.
They stole some money.
The police were after them.
They tried to escape.
They didn't want to be caught.
So they drove their car over a cliff.

Brad with Geena Davies in *Thelma and Louise*.

Brad was only in *Thelma and Louise*
for 14 minutes.
He only earned $6,000.
But everyone wanted to know his name.
Who was the good-looking young actor
in the cowboy hat ?

After appearing in *Thelma and Louise*,
Brad was voted 'The Sexiest Man Alive'.
Every Hollywood director
wanted him
to star in their next film.

7   Not Just a Pretty Face

Over the next few years
Brad Pitt made lots of great movies.

He has worked
with lots of famous actors:
David Duchovny (*Kalifornia*)
Tom Cruise (*Interview With a Vampire*)
Morgan Freeman (*Seven*)
Bruce Willis (*Twelve Monkeys*)
Robert de Niro (*Sleepers*)
Harrison Ford (*The Devil's Own*)
Anthony Hopkins (*Meet Joe Black*)
Edward Norton (*Fight Club*)
Julia Roberts (*The Mexican*)
Robert Redford (*The Spy Game*)
George Clooney (*Ocean's Eleven*)

Brad Pitt may be good-looking,
but he is also a very good actor.

Brad with George Clooney in *Ocean's Eleven*.

He wants to be remembered for his acting,
not just his good looks.

Brad has acted in some unusual films.
He has played some unusual parts.
In *Seven* he played a policeman.
In *Kalifornia* he played a killer.
In *Seven Years in Tibet* he played an explorer.
In *Interview with a Vampire* he played a vampire.
In *Meet Joe Black* he played Death.
In *True Romance* he played a drug-addict.
In *Snatch* he played a bare-knuckle boxer
called 'One Punch Mickey'.
In *Being John Malkovich* he played himself!

One of his most famous characters is
Jeffrey in *Twelve Monkeys*.
Jeffrey wanted to free all the animals in the zoo.
He talks very fast.
He is a little bit crazy.
It was a fantastic part.

His favourite character is Tyler in *Fight Club*.

Tyler is a rebel.

He likes fighting.

He always gets what he wants.

He is crazy.

But Tyler doesn't really exist!

Brad as his favourite character – Tyler in *Fight club*.

8   Blue-eyed Boy

Women all over the world fancy Brad Pitt.
Young women think he is handsome.
Old women think he is handsome.
Gay men think he is handsome.
His blue eyes
and toothpaste-advert smile are famous.

A stalker once broke into Brad's house.
She put on his clothes
and waited for him to find her.

Brad was once photographed
sunbathing nude on a beach.
The photos appeared in *Playgirl*.

He has dated some of the most
beautiful Hollywood film-stars.
He has been out with stars like
Demi Moore, Nicole Appleton and Uma Thurman.

Brad with ex-girlfriend Gwyneth Paltrow.

He started going out with
some of his famous girlfriends
when they made films together:
Jill Schoelen (*Cutting Glass*)
Juliette Lewis (*Kalifornia*)
Geena Davies (*Thelma and Louise*)
Gwyneth Paltrow (*Seven*).

Brad and Gwyneth Paltrow
were together for nearly three years.
when he was away filming
he rang her on his mobile phone
for two hours every day.
The phone bill was $65,000!
Brad asked her to marry him,
but she said no!
She said she was too young.
He asked her again.
She said no again.
He asked her again.
She said no again.
The fourth time he asked,
she said yes.

He bought her a diamond ring for $35 000.
They bought three houses next to each other.
One for Brad,
one for Gwyneth
and one for all their staff.
They bought a $1 million flat in London.
They were planning the wedding
when Brad suddenly broke off the engagement.
He decided he didn't want to get married after all.

9 Jennifer

In 1998, Brad started going out with
Jennifer Aniston.
She is also a famous actress.
She plays Rachel in *Friends*.
Brad has also appeared in *Friends*.

They went on holiday together
to Africa, Mexico and Spain.

On 29 July 2000,
Brad and Jennifer were married.
The wedding took place in a huge white tent
at a mansion by the sea.
There were 200 guests,
including lots of Hollywood stars
and the cast of *Friends*.
There were four bands and a choir.
The fireworks cost $7 000.
The flowers cost $25 000.
The whole wedding cost a million dollars.

Brad with his wife, Jennifer Aniston.

Fans tried to take photographs
from boats and helicopters.

It is hard to be private
when you are famous.

Fans and photographers follow Brad
wherever he goes.
He and Jennifer once went shopping.
A huge crowd followed them.
They had to ask the police to take them home.

Brad and Jennifer now live in Beverly Hills
in Southern California.
Their house cost 13 million dollars.
It has several tennis courts
and a private cinema.
They have also bought an
11 million dollar holiday home by the sea.

10 Did You Know?

Brad doesn't eat meat.
His favourite food is pizza.
His favourite drinks are coffee and beer.
He collects furniture.
He smokes.
He enjoys cycling, rock-climbing and tennis.
He and Jennifer enjoy cross-skating.
This is like skiing on roller-blades.

He likes listening to loud rock music,
especially Jimi Hendrix.
His favourite films are
Planet of the Apes and *Saturday Night Fever.*
He once gave 100,000 dollars
to a children's museum.
He used to keep lizards and wild-cats.
He hates sharks and spiders.

Brad learned to ride a horse
for *Legends of the Fall*.
He learned to use guns for *Seven*.
He learned to box for *Snatch*.
When he was filming *Snatch*,
Brad wasn't allowed to wash for three days
in case his tattoos came off!

11 Brad's Films

Thelma and Louise (1991)
A River Runs Through It (1992)
Kalifornia (1993)
Interview with a Vampire (1994)
Legends of the Fall (1994)
Seven (1995)
Twelve Monkeys (1996)
Seven Years in Tibet (1997)
Meet Joe Black (1998)
Fight Club (1999)
Snatch (2000)
The Mexican (2001)
The Spy Game (2001)
Ocean's Eleven (2001)

12 How Well Do You Know Brad?

1   What is Brad's birthday?

2   Where was Brad born?

3   What was the name of his first car?

4   What was his nick-name at school?

5   Who starred in *Thelma Louise*?

6   Who co-starred in *Twelve Monkeys*?

7   What does Brad like collecting?

8   Which famous actress did Brad nearly marry?

9   What part does Brad play in *Meet Joe Black*?

10   What is his wife's name?